M000195387

SOUL SET FREE

STUDY GUIDE

JOHN LINDELL

SOUL SET FREE

STUDY GUIDE

CHARISMA
HOUSE

Most Charisma House Book Group products are available at special quantity discounts for bulk purchase for sales promotions, premiums, fund-raising, and educational needs. For details, call us at (407) 333-0600 or visit our website at www.charismahouse.com

SOUL SET FREE STUDY GUIDE by John Lindell
Published by Charisma House
Charisma Media/Charisma House Book Group
600 Rinehart Road
Lake Mary, Florida 32746

This book or parts thereof may not be reproduced in any form, stored in a retrieval system, or transmitted in any form by any means—electronic, mechanical, photocopy, recording, or otherwise—without prior written permission of the publisher, except as provided by United States of America copyright law.

Unless otherwise noted, all Scripture quotations are taken the Holy Bible, English Standard Version. Copyright © 2001 by Crossway Bibles, a division of Good News Publishers. Used by permission.

Scripture quotations marked AMP are from the Amplified Bible. Copyright © 2015 by The Lockman Foundation. Used by permission. www.Lockman.org

Scripture quotations marked CEV are from the Contemporary English Version, copyright © 1995 by the American Bible Society. Used by permission.

Scripture quotations marked CEB are from the Common English Bible, copyright © 2010. All rights reserved.

Scripture quotations marked CJB are from the Complete Jewish Bible, copyright © 1998 by David H. Stern. All rights reserved.

Scripture quotations marked ERV are from the Easy-to Read Version, copyright © 2006 by Bible League International.

Scripture quotations marked GW are taken from GOD'S WORD®, © 1995 God's Word to the Nations. Used by permission of Baker Publishing Group.

Scripture quotations marked MSG are from *The Message: The Bible in Contemporary English*, copyright © 1993, 1994, 1995, 1996, 2000, 2001, 2002. Used by permission of NavPress Publishing Group.

Scripture quotations marked NIV are taken from the Holy Bible, New International Version®, NIV®. Copyright © 1973, 1978, 1984, 2011 by Biblica, Inc.®. Used by permission. All rights reserved worldwide. New International Version® and NIV® are registered trademarks of Biblica, Inc. Use of either trademark for the offering of goods or services requires the prior written consent of Biblica US, Inc.

Scripture quotations marked NLT are from the Holy Bible, New Living Translation, copyright © 1996, 2004, 2007. Used by permission of Tyndale House Publishers, Inc., Wheaton, IL 60189. All rights reserved.

Scripture quotations marked PHILLIPS are from *The New Testament in Modern English*, Revised Edition. Copyright © 1958, 1960, 1972 by J. B. Phillips. Macmillan Publishing Co. Used by permission.

Scripture quotations marked TLB are from The Living Bible. Copyright © 1971. Used by permission of Tyndale House Publishers, Inc., Wheaton, IL 60189. All rights reserved.

Copyright © 2019 by John Lindell
All rights reserved

Visit the author's website at jamesriver.church and soulsetfree.live.

Library of Congress Cataloging-in-Publication Data:
An application to register this book for cataloging has been submitted to the Library of Congress.
International Standard Book Number: 978-1-62999-704-9
E-book ISBN: 978-1-62999-712-4

While the author has made every effort to provide accurate internet addresses at the time of publication, neither the publisher nor the author assumes any responsibility for errors or for changes that occur after publication. Further, the publisher does not have any control over and does not assume any responsibility for author or third-party websites or their content.

19 20 21 22 23 — 987654321
Printed in the United States of America

CONTENTS

A NOTE FROM PASTOR JOHN

WE CALL THE gospel good news because that's exactly what it is; however, in decades of pastoral ministry I have observed that many Christians believe it is just "sort of good news." The reason the soul-freeing magnitude of the gospel hasn't taken hold of their hearts is that they have never fully understood the enormity of the gift they have received. That's why I wrote the book *Soul Set Free*, because in reality the news about what Jesus Christ did for us and what He is in fact still doing is the best news the world has ever heard!

What can close the gap between you feeling the gospel is just sort of good news and you knowing deep down that it is the best possible news you could ever hear? How do you go from living under the soul-crushing weight of self-justification to a life-giving relationship with the living God? What is the key that can unlock your soul and transform a life that is burdened, heavy with guilt, and weighed down by your faults? How do you stop striving to live a victorious life? How do you stop merely surviving? In a word the answer is grace.

It is grace that sets Christianity apart from every other world religion. It is grace that is the key to a life liberated to walk fully in God's purpose and plan. God's grace is far bigger, better, and wilder than you could ever imagine!

Grace says that everything you have ever needed has been done already for you by Christ. Grace says you can lay the burden down and let people off the hook—even let yourself off the hook. Grace says there is nothing else you have to do to make yourself right or righteous. Grace says you are set free!

So step out into grace with me. In fact don't just take a step; dive in, believing grace changes everything—most of all, you!

HOW TO USE THIS STUDY GUIDE

INDIVIDUAL STUDY

If you are working through this study on your own, you will need the book *Soul Set Free*. As you read the related chapters in the book and then answer the questions in each session, ask God to speak to you and transform you. Keep a Bible handy as well. Take your time as you go through the material, and be honest as you respond. Allow the Holy Spirit to free you as you grasp a new understanding of grace.

BIBLE STUDIES AND SMALL GROUPS

If you are a leader, have everyone obtain a copy of *Soul Set Free* and this study guide. Each session in this guide corresponds to a chapter or chapters in the book. Ask your members to read the chapters first, then complete the questions in the study guide. Doing both will help them fully participate and grow in grace.

Each session contains an opening question to help your group shake off the distractions of the day and focus in on the subject matter. A personal word from the author introduces the material, followed by reflection questions. This *Soul Set Free* study guide covers Romans 1–8, so discussion questions from the Bible reading are next. Each session closes by challenging the group members to believe for change by integrating these truths into their lives. The final section, "In My Life," is the same for all sessions and gives a moment for the members to hear from God and commit to life modifications.

Each week lead the group in a discussion using the questions from the week's session. You will probably not have time for all of them, so choose the ones you want to focus on.

Close the study with a creative time of prayer. Remind everyone to prepare for the next week by reading the book and working through the guide.

Encourage your members to take their time as they go through the material. Ask them to carefully consider the questions and approach each one honestly so the Holy Spirit can truly free them through a full understanding of grace.

THERE IS GRACE FOR YOU

THIS SESSION IS a companion to chapters 1 and 2 of *Soul Set Free: Why Grace Is More Liberating Than You Believe.*

FOCUS IN

▶ You have heard the old hymn "Amazing Grace." What does *grace* mean to you?

A PERSONAL WORD

"I'm a messed-up dude," I told my wife, Debbie. Sitting in the airplane on our way to a Florida vacation, I could tell that something just wasn't right. Despite the fact that I had pastored James River Church in Springfield, Missouri, for twenty-five years and that fifteen thousand gathered to worship there every week, I had to admit I wasn't sure if I actually loved God the Father. I wanted to love Him, but I wasn't sure that I did. And I certainly didn't feel as if He could really love me. I felt a polite distance between us.

As I sat there reflecting on this, I said to Debbie, "I just don't feel like I really get it. I don't *get* grace." I needed to get it. After all, I was a pastor. But the grace that I knew as a concept and a doctrine, the grace I even preached, seemed just out of my grasp. I felt like an outsider, pressing my face up against the glass, looking in, observing, longing.

Debbie, on the other hand, oozes grace. It was not hard for her to enjoy her walk with God. For me, it was always a matter of hard work and discipline. For Debbie, doing life with God was less structured, more relational, and a whole lot more relaxed. For me, doing more than what was required was good, and doing too much was just about right.

REFLECTION

▶ Whose experience with God do you relate to more, Pastor John's or Debbie's? Why?

▶ Whether you relate more to Pastor John or Debbie, do you feel there is something missing in your love for God? Do you grasp His love for you? How would you describe what is missing?

▶ Pastor John began by telling us how he felt about God the Father. What is the first feeling you have when God the Father comes to mind?

▶ If you had to describe a weakness in your relationship with God, what would it be?

After that airplane ride Pastor John began to study God the Father and His love for people, including himself. Over time he realized that grace is the framework by which the love of the Father is explored and expressed. It humbled him to realize it had taken so long for him to get this understanding of grace.

You may know what grace is, and you surely have experienced it. But a true understanding of grace has the power to heal your eyes so nothing looks the same. You are able to view Scripture, the world around you, and perhaps most of all yourself through healed eyes. Grace is a whole different way of seeing the world.

▶ Pastor John admitted that even after decades of pastoring, he needed a deeper understanding of God's grace for himself. Please take a moment to write out a prayer to God asking for a clearer view of His grace during this study.

▶ What questions do you have about God's grace? What do you want to understand better about His grace?

▶ Let yourself dream for a moment. What would your life be like if you truly grasped and fully believed the following statements?

God is not surprised by your failures.

God is committed to sticking with you all the way through to complete transformation.

When you fall, you don't have to start from zero again.

No one could love you more than God does.

Grasping God's amazing grace changed Pastor John's life, and it will change yours too.

FROM THE BIBLE

Read Acts 9:1–19.

This study is based on the book of Romans—Paul the apostle's greatest work, the Magna Carta of grace. During his quest Pastor John dove in to this book with his defenses down and his heart wide open. Suddenly the good news that Paul wrote about really became good news. Pastor John caught a glimpse of how God sees him. And his life changed, just as Paul's life changed on the road to Damascus.

Paul, then known as Saul, was the candidate least likely to grasp grace. As a Jew of the Jews he had the right bloodline and a white-hot zeal for God. He had studied the Torah (the Hebrew law) under a well-known rabbi, and he was an expert in the law. This gave him the vantage point from which to judge who was doing it wrong and who was doing it right.

Saul set his zeal against this new cult that claimed the crucified Jesus of Nazareth had risen from the dead and was the long-expected Jewish Messiah. He was trying to eradicate those who believed in Jesus when God met with him on the road to Damascus, blinding him and revealing Himself as Jesus. Saul was left sitting in a house, unable to see, not eating or drinking, and no doubt overwhelmed by his experience.

God sent a Christ follower named Ananias to Saul to heal him and tell him of God's purpose and plans for him. Ananias was afraid to go at first because of Saul's reputation for arresting disciples of Christ. But he obeyed God and even greeted Saul by saying, "Brother Saul." And the moment Saul was accepted and called "brother," he was able to see. Grace, for Saul and for us, is a new way of seeing.

Grace changed the trajectory of Paul's life. God saw him not as he was but as he would become. His passion for killing Christians became a passion for Christ. The terrorist of the early church became a terrorist to the powers of darkness. Because of his encounter with Christ's grace, he changed the world as we know it.

► Why was Paul an unlikely candidate for grace? What did he depend on before he met Christ? What changed for him after he met Christ?

► We just read about Paul's transformation story. Which of the following best describes where you are in your walk with Christ?

- I grew up in church but never really said yes to God for myself.

- I'm a new believer.

- I've been going to church for several years.

- I've been a Christian for many years.

- I'm in a different situation:

► Briefly share your transformation story.

BELIEVE FOR CHANGE

▶ Though you have experienced grace from God, do you believe there is more to grace than you understand? Which of the following statements do you want to believe and receive about grace?

- No matter who I am or where I have come from or what I have done, there is grace for me.

- If I feel unworthy or that I don't measure up, there is grace for me.

- If I struggle with legalism (following rules) and judgment, or if I am always trying to earn God's approval, there is grace for me.

- If I have a hard time letting go of the past or letting go of a hurt and forgiving the person who hurt me, there is grace for me.

- If I am fighting an addiction or a habitual sin, there is grace for me.

- If I struggle with getting God's truths from my head into my heart, and if I'm not quite able to trust God and feel free, there is grace for me.

▶ Which of these was most meaningful to you? Why?

Grace really does cover you in all the ways you need to be covered. It empowers you to change, to grow, and even to be formed into the likeness of Christ. Yet grace doesn't just cover us—it transforms us. Grace can revolutionize you if you are a new Christian or a seasoned believer. You will shed the skin of any joyless Christianity that feels impossible to live. And grace will help you love God more as you realize how much He loves you.

▶ What are you looking forward to most in this study?

IN MY LIFE

Take a moment to close your eyes and ask the Lord to speak to your heart as you respond to the following questions.

▶ What stands out to you from the study this week?

▶ What adjustments will you make in your life because of what you have learned?

▶ How will your relationship with God and your relationships with others change?

THE BEST NEWS YOU'VE NEVER HEARD

THIS SESSION IS a companion to chapter 3 of *Soul Set Free: Why Grace Is More Liberating Than You Believe*.

FOCUS IN

▶ The word *gospel* means good news. What news could you receive that would be so exciting you would immediately call your friends and tell them about it?

A PERSONAL WORD

I randomly read about Johnny Cash in several books that came out shortly after his passing. Cash didn't just sing about living hard—he actually did his share of it, including marital affairs and on-again, off-again drug and alcohol addiction. He was a man well acquainted with the bottom, and God was waiting for him there.

If you are like me—the kind of person who thinks that

I do my part and God does His part—the story of Johnny Cash may be shocking to you. What shocked me was not his dark side or wild lifestyle. It was the message that Johnny Cash portrayed, which was more like "God does His part. Period."

Johnny's life led me to see that grace is a whole lot bigger and a great deal wider than I had been led to believe. Cash writes, "My separation from [God], the deepest and most ravaging of the various kinds of loneliness I'd felt over the years, seemed finally complete. It wasn't. I thought I'd left Him, but He hadn't left me. I felt something very powerful start to happen to me, a sensation of utter peace, clarity, and sobriety.... Then my mind started focusing on God."[1] What a remarkable picture of grace!

REFLECTION

▶ What is your gut reaction to this story about Johnny Cash? What is shocking about God's grace in this story?

▶ Have you felt that the gospel of grace means you do your part and God does His part? If so, what is your part, and what is His part?

Pastor John describes the grace of the gospel in these unusual ways:

- Grace is not for the faint of heart or for the refined but for rogues and rebels.

- Grace is wild; it refuses to be hemmed in by either our human standards or our religious tradition.

- Grace is messy, and it sovereignly disrupts lives.

- Grace is untamed, and for rule followers it can border on reckless.

▶ What is your response to these descriptions of grace? Which one do you relate to the most? Why? Which one is the most shocking to you? Describe why.

▶ What would it take for you to allow yourself to receive this kind of grace? What obstacles hold you back?

FROM THE BIBLE

Read Romans 1:1–17.

The big idea from the Book of Romans is the same big idea that changed Paul's life on the road to Damascus. When Paul writes to the Romans years after his experience, he encapsulates his message like this:

> For I am not ashamed of the gospel, for it is the power of God for salvation to everyone who believes, to the

> Jew first and also to the Greek. For in it the righteous-
> ness of God is revealed from faith to faith, as it is
> written, "The righteous shall live by faith."
> —Romans 1:16–17

▸ The two words that animate everything Paul does and says
are *the gospel*. The gospel changed Paul, and the same good
news changes us.

The gospel of grace is God's work. It is His idea. God has
done all the heavy lifting. The gospel is not contingent on
anything we have done or not done. The gospel is all about
what Jesus has done for us.

Many of us see in the gospel what we must...

DO

Paul learned that the gospel was the proclamation of what
God has...

DONE

▸ Which of the two words—*do* and *done*—honestly describes
your view of the gospel?

▶ How does the simple two-letter difference between these two words make all the difference in how you see God? Your relationship with God? Your view of grace?

▶ How would your life be different if your trust was 100 percent in what God has already DONE rather than in what you need to DO?

The gospel is also a prescription for what ails us. It contains the very healing of God. We can take one dose, and it will change us for eternity.

▶ When is the last time you took a prescription? What was it for? How did it help?

▶ How is the gospel of grace like a prescription for you? What has the gospel healed in your life?

BELIEVE FOR CHANGE

God was not caught off guard by the failures of humankind. The gospel was not an afterthought. He knew that we would hurt ourselves and others, that we would violate His laws. Before any of it happened, God had a plan to get us, His sons and daughters, back.

As we receive the gospel of grace, we can start to see ourselves as God sees us. Read the following statements and notice your reaction to each one.

- God is excited about you. He is excited to know you and for you to know Him.

- God delights in you—not because of anything you have done but simply because you exist.

- God loves you precisely where you are and how you are—exactly as you were made.

- God has been crazy about you every minute of your life.

- God sees things in you that you cannot see.

- God sees you and knows you exactly where you are and how you are, and He loves you madly.

- God wanted you and chose you.

- God has always known you, watched over you, and cared for you.

- God's love surrounds you, covers you, and calls out for you by name.

▶ Which statements did you have an easy time believing?

▶ Which statements were difficult for you to accept? Why?

▶ We cannot take the gospel of grace too far because God has already taken it farther! What would it be like to fall into this ocean of grace? Write a prayer to God, noting any hesitations you have and asking Him to show you the fullness of His gospel of grace.

IN MY LIFE

Take a moment to close your eyes and ask the Lord to speak to your heart as you respond to the following questions.

▶ What stands out to you from the study this week?

▶ What adjustments will you make in your life because of what you have learned?

▶ How will your relationship with God and your relationships with others change?

THE BAD NEWS

THIS SESSION IS a companion to chapter 4 of *Soul Set Free: Why Grace Is More Liberating Than You Believe.*

FOCUS IN

▶ Many twelve-step recovery programs ask their members to share their names and admit their problems: "Hi. My name is John, and I am a sinner." Now you try. How did this make you feel?

A PERSONAL WORD

We all realize that something is not right with this world, and we know we are complicit in its greed, violence, and injustice. In our honest moments we know we have played a role in this unjust world, that we are a long way from Jesus' vision of a people who value meekness and humility. Since we recognize that we are not in alignment with God's good purpose for creation, we try to justify ourselves and even charm our way out of any consequences.

This recently happened with my son Brandon and his wife, Beth. When they arrived at the airport for a trip, Brandon realized he didn't have his ID. He googled on his phone and found out that you can sometimes get through airport security using mail with your address on it as a form of ID. So he madly tore through his car, finding a few coffee-stained bills. Remarkably, the nice TSA folks let him through.

Brandon doubted that he would have the same luck on the way back, so he had a friend break into his house, find his ID, and overnight it to him. When Brandon opened the package, he discovered that his ID had expired and even had a hole punched through it. But somehow, with this ID and his church employee ID card, he made it through the checkpoint.

We do the same thing with God, scrambling breathlessly for some shred of evidence that might validate us. We parade our list of accomplishments before Him, thinking that we will earn brownie points and somehow make it into God's good graces. But no matter how hard we try, we don't have any credentials that will justify us.

REFLECTION

▶ Can you think of a time when you narrowly avoided an unpleasant consequence that you really deserved?

► What are some reasons you might give God to convince Him that you are really a good person?

► If you asked some unsaved friends or coworkers why God should allow them into His heaven, what reasons might they give? Will these reasons get them into heaven?

In Jeremiah the Lord says, "The heart is deceitful above all things, and desperately sick; who can understand it?" (Jer. 17:9).

► Why is it important to understand that we are sinners before we can fully appreciate what Jesus did for us?

Paul writes in Romans 1 that creation itself bears witness to the splendor and majesty of God (v. 20). From the starry cosmos to the intricacies of our own bodies, all the staggering beauty and spectacular craftsmanship screams to us of a Designer. So when we choose to worship something besides God, we can be held accountable for this idolatry. We search for something or someone other than God to fulfill us, to give us purpose and meaning. We use our idols to gratify ourselves instead of looking to the only One who can satisfy us.

▶ What are some ways you try to gratify yourself outside of God?

▶ Where do you look for meaning and purpose outside of God?

C. S. Lewis writes in *The Great Divorce* that hell is locked from the inside. "There are only two kinds of people in the end," Lewis concludes, "those who say to God, 'Thy will be done,' and those to whom God says, in the end, 'Thy will be done.'"[1]

▶ What if in the end God gave you what you regularly chased after, often chose, and what you "really" wanted? What would that be like for you?

FROM THE BIBLE

Read Romans 2:1–13.

▶ In this passage Paul calls us on the carpet for judging others when we commit the very same wrongs ourselves. Have you ever compared yourself favorably with someone you thought to be morally worse off than you? What gave you that sense of moral superiority?

▶ Paul followed all the Jewish laws and kept all the rules, yet his moral superiority never transformed his heart. Why are we so quick to judge another in an area in which we are strong?

▶ Do we also judge others in areas in which we are weak and unsuccessful? Why or why not?

▶ Why does God warn us about the dangers of judging others?

▶ Paul said a day of wrath is coming when the righteous judgment of God will be revealed (v. 5). What is your gut reaction to the word *wrath*?

The wrath of God is not arbitrary or impulsive. It is not emotional, petty, or punitive. Rather, in Romans 2 it is bound up in the natural consequences of certain kinds of choices. God isn't trying to make sure everyone gets what they deserve. In fact He is constantly interrupting the natural cycle of cause and effect with grace. Still, we get to choose. God won't drag anyone kicking and screaming into some kind of eternal bliss without his or her consent.

In the Gospel of John we read, "Whoever believes in the Son has eternal life; whoever does not obey the Son shall not see life, but the wrath of God remains on him" (John 3:36). Those who have not been forgiven and justified through Christ are under the wrath of God already. But when we come to Christ, we are justified and no longer under God's wrath.

God is actively opposed and wholly hostile to evil. He will not condone it or come to terms with it. The justice of God is actually a manifestation of the love of God because all that is exploitive, oppressive, and abusive must be brought under judgment for things to be made right. God, who is relentlessly committed to loving and restoring His creation, must judge the world.

▶ Perhaps you grew up with a father or father figure who blew up in anger or was erratic or abusive or out of control, taking out his frustrations on the people around him, including you. If so, list some ways that God, even in His wrath, is different from that.

Because God is so passionately loving toward His children, He is radically opposed to sin and evil. He cannot help but abhor that which brings His children harm.

▸ How does it make you feel that God wants to protect you from evil, even if it involves the manifestation of His wrath in judgment?

▸ What would it be like to live in a world that was, as author N. T. Wright states, "put to rights"? (See "The Wrath of God" section in chapter 4 in *Soul Set Free*.) What would be removed from it? What would be added to it?

BELIEVE FOR CHANGE

We are far more prone to self-deception, selfishness, and outright meanness than we know. That bent toward self runs right down to our bones.

God takes what we do seriously because He takes us seriously. Judgment matters because we matter. Judgment has weight because we have weight with God.

▸ How might knowing that God gives your life and choices so much weight affect your next choice, your next action?

The only way to experience radical transformation is to completely give up on justifying ourselves. We must throw ourselves completely into the arms of the God who loves us at our worst.

▶ What are the things you do or omit doing that make you feel the guiltiest?

▶ If you were the loving parent of one who just made this list describing himself at his worst, what would you say to your child?

In the end we fall upon the love and grace of God. When we get to the end of ourselves, the story of God's outrageous grace can begin.

▶ Most résumés list the qualifications of the job hunter. If you were writing a résumé to apply for God's grace, what would you write about yourself?

▶ How does it make you feel to know that when it comes to God's grace, your qualifications don't matter?

IN MY LIFE

Take a moment to close your eyes and ask the Lord to speak to your heart as you respond to the following questions.

▶ What stands out to you from the study this week?

▶ What adjustments will you make in your life because of what you have learned?

▶ How will your relationship with God and your relationships with others change?

THE GIFT OF A LIFETIME

THIS SESSION IS a companion to chapters 5 and 6 *of Soul Set Free: Why Grace Is More Liberating Than You Believe.*

FOCUS IN

► Think of a time when you forgave someone and your relationship was restored. Then think of a time when you forgave someone, but you never wanted to see that person again. What was the difference?

A PERSONAL WORD

My son David has three boys and one girl. Though David's daughter is named Henley, he calls her Boo. She's a unique mix of lovable sweetness and daredevil. Not long ago she exhibited her daring side by hitting one of her older brothers. David sat down with her and asked her, "Boo, why did you hit your brother?" She answered with a glint in her eye,

"Because I wanted to." It was hilarious because she's cute and delightful, but she answered like a cold-blooded gangster!

This is the heart of our sin problem: we want to sin. We have seen the darkness, especially in our own hearts. Yes, God forgives us, but forgiveness is not all we need. We are in need of nothing short of utter transformation. We need to be changed from the inside out, and we can't do it ourselves. All our effort and our good intentions cannot yield success.

Paul reveals the radical answer to our sin: justification. Justification is a gift, and it cannot be earned. It is received by believing, and by believing alone. The stark backdrop of the bad news of our sinful natures only makes the glory of the good news shine all the brighter.

REFLECTION

> Justification is the act of God whereby He forgives the unsaved person's sin and imputes/credits/assigns to them the righteousness of Christ when through faith they believe.

▶ Choose the important words in the previous sentence. How would you explain this concept to a young child?

▶ What stands out to you about justification? What is the most significant part of this description to you?

► Justification starts with God taking the initiative. How should that frame the way we see salvation and God's desire for relationship with us?

► Forgiveness is letting go of a debt, letting someone off the hook for their wrongs, and refusing to seek retribution. When you think of God forgiving you like that, what is your reaction?

Our sin problem is far more profound than any particular deeds we commit; it is a way of being in the world without God—a way of attempting to live our lives without being connected to our divine source. Sin is not just about actions that need to be pardoned but about sickness that needs to be healed.

► Do you think of sin as things you do or don't do? Or do you think of sin as something much deeper? What does it mean to you that sin is a sickness that needs to be healed?

Justification means that God's righteousness has been credited to you. You are now the righteousness of God in Christ (2 Cor. 5:21). Other Bible translations or paraphrases describe righteousness in this verse in these ways:

- "be made good with the goodness of God" (Phillips)

- "be made acceptable to Him and placed in a right relationship with Him by His gracious lovingkindness" (amp)

- "be made right with God through Christ" (nlt)

- "make us acceptable to God" (cev)

- "[Christ] poured God's goodness into us" (tlb)

► Which of these descriptions speaks to you the most? Why?

► Justification means that when God looks at you, He doesn't see your sin. Instead He sees the righteousness of Christ. How could fully understanding that truth affect your life?

FROM THE BIBLE

Read Romans 4 and Ephesians 1:3–5.

Though we are not justified (made right with God) through our works, God requires one thing of us to receive this free gift of justification: faith.

Israel's first bona fide rock star was Abraham. He was one of the heroes of the Old Testament and the father of the faith to devout Jews. According to Paul, the reason God was able to powerfully use Abraham—promising him a great name, a great nation, many sons and daughters, and that all the families of the earth would be blessed through him—was that Abraham *believed* what God promised him. Though Abraham got a lot wrong, he got this right. He just believed God.

► Write out Romans 4:3. Then write it again, putting in your name instead of Abraham's. What came to mind as you were writing it with your name?

► Having read what Paul writes in Romans 4:10–11, how does knowing that you are justified through faith keep you from falling into the trap of works-based righteousness? If righteousness comes only through faith and not by the things we do, why should you still pray and read the Bible?

► After reading Romans 4:11 and Ephesians 1:3–5, what is the first thought that comes to mind when you hear that "long before he laid down earth's foundations, he had us in mind, had settled on us as the focus of his love, to be made whole and holy by his love" (Eph. 1:4, MSG)? How does knowing this truth actually encourage you to live a godly life?

▶ Abraham took God at His word. He completely trusted in God's promises. What are some instances when Abraham obeyed God without any explanation?

▶ When Abraham was resting on God's promise to give him and Sarah a child, what does Romans 4:18–22 say he did?

Abraham was "fully persuaded that God had power to do what he had promised" (Rom. 4:21, NIV). Faith believes that God is not only powerful enough to do what He says He will do but also fully trustworthy to be depended on to do it.

▶ Paul maintains that the way to God in the Old Testament days was the same as the way to God in the New Testament: through believing. Think of a problem or some trouble you are going through right now. Are you fully persuaded that God can do what He has promised? Do you trust Him to do it? How can you demonstrate, as Abraham did, that you trust Him?

Abraham hoped against hope for Sarah to have the promised child (v. 18). In other words, he had no reason to hope based on what he saw or felt or the evidence around him. He was about one hundred, and she was around ninety. But He still had hope—hope in the word of God and the character of God. That was enough!

▶ Have you been praying for anything for which you are hoping against hope? Is there a promise from God that you are still believing will happen? Write out what you are hoping against hope for. Then give glory to God for the answer as Abraham did.

Faith is not denial. Abraham didn't deny the facts of the situation. Faith is not blind, but it is a different way of seeing. Faith doesn't give us a script or a map or a clear set of instructions. Faith is just trusting the character of the One who guides us as we go. Faith looks beyond the problem to the promise, and beyond the promise to the Person.

▶ In what way does knowing these things about faith set you free to believe? What misconceptions did you have about faith that you can let go of?

This kind of faith that Abraham had was credited to him as righteousness. He was not a perfect man, just a trusting one.

▶ Have you been doing anything to try to convince God to answer your prayers? What have you tried? How does faith make all this effort null and void?

BELIEVE FOR CHANGE

We often make things harder for ourselves than we need to. We can turn the idea of faith into a legalistic enterprise that depends on our efforts. We ask ourselves, "Do I have enough faith? How can I get my faith from 67 percent to 73 percent?" Sometimes we put more emphasis on our faith than on the One we have faith in.

▶ Have you ever struggled to have more faith in a situation? Did you depend more on your faith than on God? How did that work out?

Jesus said that we only need faith as small as a mustard seed to move mountains (Matt. 17:20). You have faith. The way to exercise it is to focus on God and give Him glory. The object of faith is God. We are told to fix our eyes "on Jesus, the pioneer and perfecter of faith" (Heb. 12:2, NIV).

▶ How can you move your gaze off yourself and onto Jesus as you wait for your answer?

Believing God takes all the focus off us and puts it on God. Why faith? Because all the glory goes to God while we do nothing!

► Is it a relief to you that none of the pressure for making something happen is on you? Write how you feel about God getting all the glory because God does all the work.

Sometimes we start out in faith, but we assume that the longer we follow Christ, the more certainty we will have. The truth is a life of faith is not a way of more certainty but of less! We will never start to know more about the path ahead. It is always about trust, not knowledge.

► Have you ever felt, even subconsciously, that faith will feel more like certainty as you mature in Christ? What is your reaction to the idea that faith will always require believing? Is that helpful?

► Based on what you've discovered in this session, make two lists, one noting what faith is and one noting what faith is not.

IN MY LIFE

Take a moment to close your eyes and ask the Lord to speak to your heart as you respond to the following questions.

► What stands out to you from the study this week?

► What adjustments will you make in your life because of what you have learned?

► How will your relationship with God and your relationships with others change?

PEACE WITH GOD

Тhis session is a companion to chapters 7 and 8 of *Soul Set Free: Why Grace Is More Liberating Than You Believe.*

FOCUS IN

▶ What is one thing in life you know for sure? Why are you so sure about it?

A PERSONAL WORD

In my years as a pastor I have noticed that too many Christians live in fear. They have the nagging sense that they might not actually be saved. When an altar call is given, deep down they feel they might need to pray "the prayer" again because they sinned since the last time an altar call was given. They wonder if they have fallen from grace and perhaps their relationship with God has been compromised. So they feel that they need to be born again, again. Maybe it will take this time, they hope.

Actually God does not make us start over every time we make a mistake. But some people struggle so much with having an assurance of salvation that it is actually damaging to them. They are constantly second-guessing their relationship with God. If salvation is always dependent on their good behavior, then it is a fragile, tenuous thing. That kind of uncertainty about their souls can infect every area of their lives, infusing anxiety into everything they do. It destroys intimacy with God.

This usually happens when people don't understand that through justification the obstacles between God and themselves have been removed. They don't realize that they have been reconciled with God, that the war is over, and that they have peace with God. All this was accomplished by God, for us, as a free gift. It is time that we start living in peace with God.

REFLECTION

Remember, justification is the act of God whereby He forgives the unsaved person's sin and imputes/credits/assigns to them the righteousness of Christ when through faith they believe. A real transaction takes place in which our status with God has been completely and irrevocably altered. Justification is a legal, binding transaction in the court of love, and peace with God has been established between us forever.

▸ Since the last session what have you thought about most regarding justification? Do you understand it better than you did before?

Romans 5:1 is a hinge scripture for the entire book of Romans.

> Therefore, since we have been justified by faith, we
> have peace with God through our Lord Jesus Christ.

This peace with God is not a psychological peace or the peace we feel when we commit something to God in prayer. This is peace that comes because the war between you and God is over. The sin in your very DNA that has caused war with God and war with yourself has been forgiven. You are justified before God.

▶ Is there a sin in your life, maybe in your past, that keeps coming to mind, that you keep wrestling with? How can you apply justification to that sin?

The sacrifice of Jesus applies to every sin you have committed in the past and anticipates every sin you might ever commit. Jesus died for all our sins—past, present, and future. Any failure that is yet to come is already covered by the sacrifice of Jesus.

▶ What is your response to this good news? Do you hesitate to believe it? Why?

Since you have peace with God, your mind can be at rest about your relationship with God.

▶ What is the main obstacle that keeps coming up between you and God? How does this truth about peace with God change that?

Since you have peace with God, you no longer have to be at the mercy of the accusations from the enemy of your soul or the accusations from inside you.

▶ What are some ways in which you have been tormented by accusations? Have you ever come into the presence of God and heard accusations in your mind? How have you been vulnerable to this in the past?

▶ What will change for you as you assimilate this truth about your peace with God into your daily life?

Since you have peace with God, sinning doesn't cancel out your relationship with God. If you were to lose your salvation when you sinned, you would have to conclude that you gained salvation because you were good. That is not the gospel. Forgiveness and justification are free gifts that are not dependent on your goodness.

> For by grace you have been saved through faith. And this is not your own doing; it is the gift of God, not a result of works, so that no one may boast.
> —EPHESIANS 2:8–9

The faith wasn't yours; the grace wasn't yours—it was all a gift of God.

► Now that you know this, what will you do the next time that sinning shakes your assurance that you are saved?

► Maybe you feel as if you fail in your prayer life or you don't share your faith enough or you don't read your Bible enough, and that guilt comes between you and God. Now that you know about justification, how can you respond to guilt like that?

► How can a lack of understanding of justification and the peace you have with God make your Christian life miserable?

It is easy to see how Paul faced objections to this teaching from people who thought that believing like this would cause abuse of grace. Some said that it would free people to sin all they wanted because all their sins were already forgiven. That is how revolutionary justification is! But God is always at work in Christians to incline their hearts to His own. If someone is indifferent to sin, has no remorse, and doesn't struggle against it, perhaps that person hasn't placed his or her faith in God's work after all.

▶ What is your reaction to the good news of forgiveness, justification, and peace with God? Does it make you want to sin more? Why or why not?

FROM THE BIBLE

Read Romans 5:12–21.

We have been talking about being saved from our sin and justified by God. But where did this sin come from? As Paul teaches about justification, he responds to this question. It is important because knowing where sin comes from answers the why questions we all have. Why is there suffering? Why do people have to die? Why is there disease and sickness?

Through the tales of two men, Adam and Jesus, Paul sums up the entire story of the human species with all its heartbreak, comedy, and loss. To understand Jesus' story, we have to understand Adam's story.

▶ Write out Romans 5:12.

▶ How did sin come into the world?

Adam and Eve started out in a lush, beautiful garden. They loved each other, they loved God, and they were naked and unashamed. The world was unspoiled, without death or chaos. Everything was theirs for the taking except the fruit from one tree—the tree of the knowledge of good and evil. In a word, it was a tree of judgment. But they didn't need to be able to judge because they lived a life depending on and trusting in God.

But one day the serpent came to Eve and, by questioning God's words to Adam and Eve, tempted her to eat from the forbidden tree. Eve then wondered if God had been holding out on them. She feared missing out on something good, and she became curious. She took the fruit from the tree and ate, and Adam did too.

And just like that, everything changed. Adam and Eve felt shame and wanted to hide. Everything looked different because, as Paul wrote, "sin came into the world." The contagion was released, and there was no going back. Now, we are all born sinners because sin has been passed down to us through Adam. In this way we all bear the likeness of our ancestral father. Like Adam and Eve, we were created in the image of God, but now we have the same proclivity toward sin that Adam had.

▶ This is a story that you have heard many times before. What seemed new to you this time?

The consequence, the penalty, for their sin was death. Death, though we accept it as unavoidable, has never felt natural or right. It was never God's idea. Now we are all subject to physical death, which is separation from the living. But spiritual death, separation between God and us, also now reigns. Last comes eternal death in the place that Jesus describes as the place of outer darkness.

Paul says that "death spread to all men because all sinned" (Rom. 5:12). Adam represented the human race, and what happened to him happened to all of us. Now each of us is born into sin and death. All of us, and even all creation, have sin sickness.

▶ Often people have one of two different opinions about our human nature. One opinion is that we are basically good but we do bad things (i.e., sin), and the other is that we are basically bad but do good things. Do you believe either of these? Why? Do either of these views of our nature line up with what the Bible teaches about humanity, sin, grace, and redemption? Explain.

▶ Can you accept that all people are born into sin because of Adam? Why is that difficult news for some people to swallow?

It's time for some good news, isn't it? Thousands of years later another man came, born as a baby in a manger. When

He was an adult, the same presence that tempted Eve tempted Him. The fate of the world hung in the balance. Unlike Adam and Eve, He was not in a lush garden but in a stark desert, worn down and emaciated. But though His body was weak, He resisted the temptation. And the world would never be the same.

▶ How does understanding Adam help us understand Christ and what He did for us?

Christ didn't just undo what Adam did; He did much more. If sin spread like a contagion into all humankind through the sin of Adam, how much more does the antidote of grace spread though those who are now in Christ? God's grace through Christ became available to all of Adam's seed who believed.

▶ If you struggle with the idea of God forgiving you for old or new sins, how does it help to know that His grace is so great that it can forgive the sins of all people who ever believed? Do you think that your sin is greater than God's grace?

The free gift of grace which flows so abundantly through Christ has brought justification (Rom. 5:16). Instead of living in the tragic story of Adam, Jesus wrote a whole new story for you to live in.

▶ Is anything holding you back from living in the justification brought about through Christ's death on the cross? If so, what can you do today to change that?

BELIEVE FOR CHANGE

▶ Write out Romans 5:1.

Take a few minutes to meditate on each part of the scripture. You will remember it that way without trying.

▶ In which situations would it be helpful to recall Romans 5:1 to better understand God's grace?

▶ What does it mean to you that you are in a whole new story now—not the tragic story of Adam but the victorious and abundant story of Christ?

IN MY LIFE

Take a moment to close your eyes and ask the Lord to speak to your heart as you respond to the following questions.

▶ What stands out to you from the study this week?

▶ What adjustments will you make in your life because of what you have learned?

▶ How will your relationship with God and your relationships with others change?

DEAD TO SIN

THIS SESSION IS a companion to chapters 9 and 10 of *Soul Set Free: Why Grace Is More Liberating Than You Believe.*

FOCUS IN

▶ When you think about the most recent funeral you attended, what are some details that come to mind?

A PERSONAL WORD

As a junior in Bible college and a newlywed, I was looking for a place for Debbie and me to live and a job to support us. We prayed and asked God to provide these. Then I got a call from a funeral director who had heard about us. He offered me a job at the funeral home as well as a place to live rent-free—in the funeral home!

When I told Debbie that my response to the man was that I had to think about it, she asked, "What is there to think about? We need a place to live, you need a job, and we'll have both." I protested, saying that I was the one who would have to work in a funeral home. But I took the job.

The first night we lived there, I was called out with the funeral director, and Debbie had to stay by herself with six individuals who weren't very talkative! I call that poetic justice.

Those of us who have been around long enough have probably lived in closer proximity to death than we would like. That is the kind of death that has reigned since Adam. But now we who have been justified in Christ are actually dead to dying because our own death has been swallowed up in Christ's death.

REFLECTION

We find ourselves on earth in the middle of a battle between light and darkness, good and evil. Real life assaults us daily with its challenges and temptations. Paul wants us to view this battle from the higher perspective of grace.

We tend to forget what we have already learned about grace in the midst of the noise of life. That's why the first thing you need to do in your battle is to remember that you are forgiven and justified. You are clothed in the righteousness of God.

► We have studied forgiveness of sin—past, present, and future—and justification by faith in Christ for several weeks now. Review what you've learned by writing out what you would say to someone who is struggling to remember what Jesus did for him.

Since Christ was raised from the dead, you too have been raised to a new life and will experience resurrection to eternal life.

► What does it mean that His story is now your story?

You don't have to engineer a victory over a foe that Christ has already defeated. You just need to rehearse His story—and our story—over and over again.

► What are some ways you can tell yourself the story of Jesus' victory over Satan, sin, and death again and again? What are some ways to do it at home? In church?

► When you sin, do you naturally rehearse what Christ did for you or do you naturally rehearse the old soundtracks of guilt and shame and blame? If you rehearse the old soundtracks, what can you do to change that?

► Paul says in 2 Corinthians, "The old has passed away; behold, the new has come" (5:17). How does this scripture come to life for you as you realize that His story is your story?

▶ The old way of doing things is what Adam and Eve did when they sinned: they hid from God. What is the new way of dealing with sin with Christ?

FROM THE BIBLE

Read Romans 6.

By the time Paul gets to Romans 6, he anticipates a question that believers might ask when the grace of God is preached in all its reckless beauty: Why does it matter how I live if I am forgiven already? Can't I just go on sinning? If grace is preached rightly in all its force and power, that question will be raised. The truth is that if people aren't raising that same question now, the gospel has not been rightly proclaimed!

Paul's response is an emphatic "No!" But his reasoning is fascinating. We can't go on sinning because in Christ we are actually dead to sin itself. The reign of sin has no power over those under the reign of grace.

▶ What are some of the characteristics of being dead? How do they apply to being dead to sin?

But how does all this work? When you were in sin, you were dead. But in Christ you are now actually dead—to sin! It has no power over you. Paul says you have been baptized into Christ Himself, which means that His death became your death. When He died to sin, you died to sin. In the same way, His resurrection became your resurrection. You now live under the dominion of grace, not sin.

Since Christ already won the victory over sin, death, and the grave, the battlefield that remains is the one in your mind—and it is a powerful one. Though we are dead to sin, we are still pulled back into the battle with sin. But we have strategies to overcome sin and walk in this new life.

▶ Paul tells us to reckon, or consider, ourselves dead to sin (Rom. 6:11). At first glance what does that mean to you?

▶ You are no longer under the dominion of sin, but you do sometimes sin. You now realize that it has no real power over you because you died to sin with Christ. How can this help you bounce back quickly when you sin?

▶ When you sin, the sense of estrangement from God can be brutal. But it is an illusion. Your stumbling does not mean separation. From what you have learned, explain why sinning is not equal to separation from God.

▶ As you remind yourself that you cannot give yourself to sin because you are dead to sin, you will gradually give sin less opportunity to battle with you. Your natural and free response to the love God has poured out on you will be to give yourself to God instead. What is a good first step toward this for you?

BELIEVE FOR CHANGE

Since you are dead to sin, Paul instructs you not to present your hands and feet and ears and voice and eyes to sin to be its instruments (Rom. 6:13). Rather, we are to present our members to God.

In 2004 at a Passion Conference Chris Tomlin sang and recorded an updated version of Frances Ridley Havergal's hymn from the 1800s consecrating herself anew to Christ. In "Take My Life and Let It Be," Havergal gives her individual members to Christ to use for His glory. As you read this or sing it, make it a prayer in which you give yourself fully to God.

> Take my life and let it be
>> Consecrated, Lord, to Thee.
>> Take my moments and my days,
>> Let them flow in endless praise.
> Take my hands and let them move
>> At the impulse of Thy love.
>> Take my feet and let them be
>> Swift and beautiful for Thee.
> Take my voice and let me sing,
>> Always, only for my King.

> Take my lips and let them be
> Filled with messages from Thee.
> Take my silver and my gold,
> Not a mite would I withhold.
> Take my intellect and use
> Every pow'r as Thou shalt choose.
> Take my will and make it Thine,
> It shall be no longer mine.
> Take my heart, it is Thine own,
> It shall be Thy royal throne.
> Take my love, my Lord, I pour
> At Thy feet its treasure store.
> Take myself and I will be
> Ever, only, all for Thee.[1]

IN MY LIFE

Take a moment to close your eyes and ask the Lord to speak to your heart as you respond to the following questions.

► What stands out to you from the study this week?

► What adjustments will you make in your life because of what you have learned?

► How will your relationship with God and your relationships with others change?

THE FRUIT OF RIGHTEOUSNESS

T HIS SESSION IS a companion to chapter 11 of *Soul Set Free: Why Grace Is More Liberating Than You Believe.*

FOCUS IN

► When you were a child, your parents or caregivers gave you tasks to do, such as making your bed or brushing your teeth. As you grew up, you decided to do many of those tasks on your own without being coerced by someone else. What caused this change?

A PERSONAL WORD

Micah was eight when his pastor father was arrested and imprisoned for embezzlement. His superhero dad had failed, so he figured he couldn't measure up either. His family stopped attending church. Even after the prison sentence was over, his father still felt inadequate regarding God, and Micah absorbed that, feeling less than other Christians.

He fought with his parents and started to drink, smoke, and do drugs. Micah found himself homeless at age sixteen. He moved in with his girlfriend, and they soon had a baby. The guilt over that pushed him further away from God. But the weight of this new responsibility also helped him get a good job in sales.

At that time, his girlfriend started attending our church. She encountered Jesus, and her life was changed. Suddenly she wanted to get baptized, serve at church, and quit having sex until they got married. Micah felt threatened. The church was stealing his happiness again. Deep down he felt he was bad and that he couldn't be part of church.

One night she left him. His inner life was in shambles. Soon he realized he wanted his girlfriend and son back, so he bought a big diamond ring and tried to propose. But before he finished, she refused. She wanted a man who loved God. So out of desperation he went to church with her.

He stood stiff as a pencil during worship and felt nothing until the message started. Then he heard the good news that Jesus died for him and would cover him with His righteousness. As he thought about all the things he had done, he was caught off guard by the feeling of unimaginable freedom. The case he had built against God shattered, and Micah gave his life to Christ. For the first time he felt free—free from sin, guilt, shame, and his own accusations. He soon married his girlfriend, and their lives began to change.

Micah discovered the love of God, and he noticed that he didn't want to do the same things anymore. He knew his sin had affected people around him. But the more he began to understand grace, the more it changed the people around him too. His dad eventually came to church and rededicated his life to Christ. Later his sister-in-law did the same, and then his mother-in-law became clean and saved too after years of addiction to drugs and alcohol.

Micah's story reveals the difference between the wages of sin and the fruit of righteousness. Not only had he borne the consequences of his actions, but when Micah tried to get his life together, all the weight and sin of his former life fell upon him. It was soul-wearying work. But after the message of grace he opened his clenched fists and received everything from God as a gift. The wages of sin brought damage to his life and those around him, but the fruit of righteousness was far more bountiful than sin.

REFLECTION

► What was your life like before you came to Christ? If you had to describe it just using several adjectives, what would they be?

► In what ways did you feel that you were under the mastery of sin? What weight was on you? How did you handle it?

Sin is a master and God is a master, but they are radically different. Everyone is under one or the other. Each offers a different set of benefits and a different destiny.

► What is the difference between being a slave to sin and a slave to righteousness?

People either live under grace or under wrath, as we have seen. Paul makes a distinction between how these masters rule over us: sin pays wages, but God gives gifts.

The world apart from God is a world of wages. You get what you earn, what you deserve, and nothing more. And what we deserve is death. "The wages of sin is death" (Rom. 6:23). The language of sin, about wages, actually has to do with work. We relentlessly reap what we sow. And ultimately we are separated from God.

Yet sin is deceptive. It feels like fun. It is pleasurable for a season. We can do what we want when we want. Sin can feel like freedom.

► Name a time when sin felt like freedom to you. How did it end up? What was the result of Micah's sin?

► When a person works, he or she receives a wage or payment for the work. In Romans 6:23 "the wages" of our sin refers to a payment. How have you seen the wages of sin affect your life or the lives of those close to you? How do those wages compare to the free gift of God?

FROM THE BIBLE

Read Romans 6:15–23.

God offers an alternative to wages of sin. God's economy is filled with grace.

▶ What was your favorite Christmas gift as a child? What did you feel when you opened the gift?

▶ What does a child do to earn Christmas gifts? What does a parent experience in giving Christmas gifts?

Salvation is the gift that keeps on giving. The moment we come to Christ, He begins to undo the damage of sin. He begins to make us new.

▶ Do you remember the feeling of everything being new, of having a fresh start with Christ? What is your best memory from that time?

▶ Write out Romans 6:22.

Some people struggle with being assured that they are truly saved. Romans 6:22 says that "the benefit you reap leads to holiness" (NIV). If you are in Christ, the natural result is growing in holiness. Your appetites change, especially your appetite for sin.

▶ Have your desires for sinful things diminished since you have been with Christ? Which of your appetites have changed?

As a Christian you are not perfect, but you are growing. That process is called sanctification. The more the love of God saturates you internally, the more your behavior aligns with the heart of God. Ultimately sanctification is nothing less than falling deeper in love. People who are in love do things they wouldn't ordinarily do because their hearts are wholly devoted to the one they love.

▶ What has changed in you because of your love for Christ?

King David wasn't perfect, but he was growing in his relationship with God. He sinned, but he was quick to repent and return to God with humility. In 1 Samuel 13:14 David is described as a man after God's own heart. David's heart belonged to God, and God knew it. Your behavior might not be perfect, but if you belong to Christ, your heart is perfectly God's.

▸ When you sin, are you quick to repent and restore your relationship with God? What do you think it means that David was "a man after God's own heart"?

BELIEVE FOR CHANGE

▸ Read Luke 15:20–24 and write out what the Father did when the broke, dirty, and sorrowful prodigal son came home.

Like the prodigal son who comes home and is immediately given his father's ring, robe, and sandals and then a lavish party, God lavishes His love upon us.

▸ What could God clothe you with to begin healing your old sin wounds? What has Christ already done to undo the damage of sin?

▸ In Romans chapter 6 Paul uses the powerful imagery of slavery to talk about our relationship both to sin and to righteousness. What does it mean that a person is a slave to either sin or righteousness?

▶ In our daily lives what are some indicators that people are allowing themselves to fall into slavery to sin? What are some things a person can do to live as a slave to righteousness?

IN MY LIFE

Take a moment to close your eyes and ask the Lord to speak to your heart as you respond to the following questions.

▶ What stands out to you from the study this week?

▶ What adjustments will you make in your life because of what you have learned?

▶ How will your relationship with God and your relationships with others change?

THE FRUSTRATION OF TRYING TO PLEASE GOD ON MY OWN

THIS SESSION IS a companion to chapters 12 and 13 of *Soul Set Free: Why Grace Is More Liberating Than You Believe.*

FOCUS IN

▶ Think of a couple whose relationship you admire as strong and healthy. What is true about their relationship? Why do you think they can love each other like that?

A PERSONAL WORD

When Debbie and I first got married, I was still a bit of a punk. While driving through South Dakota on our honeymoon, I missed an exit. Seeing a median crossing about a quarter mile up the road, I decide to use it to turn around. Debbie, who followed the rules, saw that the posted sign said Authorized Vehicles Only. She said, "John, you can't do that."

I told her it was no big deal. "Debbie! We live in a country with a government of the people, by the people, and for the people. I'm one of the people...and I'm authorizing myself!" My self-righteous statement was followed by a deafening silence.

We were headed for a mall. As soon as we arrived, Debbie jumped out, walked into the mall, and left me sitting in the food court for the next hour and a half. I realized I had a long way to go! I learned what not to do as a husband. Since then I have grown to be less careless and more thoughtful.

As Debbie and I do life together, I don't follow some kind of marriage rule book. After all these years I know what pleases Debbie and what disappoints her. I don't want to intentionally hurt her. That desire doesn't come from a sense of duty or drudgery. I want to do what brings her joy!

Debbie loves fresh flowers, so I bring her a bouquet almost every week. It brings a smile to her face, but it is also a regular reminder of how much I love her. That's how following Jesus was intended to work. It is not about obligation and ritual. It's a love story!

Paul writes about the relationship between Christ and the church as a marriage. Love calls us to get lost in serving and caring for each other. In this kind of relationship there is safety, not fear. That's what it means to live under grace.

REFLECTION

As Christians we start out in love with Christ, but then we tend to wander back into a rules-oriented outlook. I describe the law as the list of the things that you should and shouldn't do. If you view keeping the law as a means of salvation, as a way to stay in right standing with God, then you have stopped walking in grace—and love.

▶ What are some things on your "should and shouldn't do" list that make you feel that you are in right standing with God when you accomplish them?

It is likely that your list included some of the classic spiritual practices such as praying, Bible reading, and attending church. Someone may have even told you that all these things are the right steps to grow in Christ, and they are wonderful practices that will be a huge source of strength for you.

The list probably also included what not to do, things such as gossiping, cursing, visiting certain places on the internet, or watching particular TV shows. Finally, when you are sufficiently loaded down with dos and don'ts, you are told to go enjoy your freedom in Christ!

It is true that striving to walk in holiness is an essential part of the Christian life, and these practices and spiritual disciplines may help you do that. After all Christ had habits such as finding time alone to pray and going to the synagogue on the Sabbath (Luke 4:16; 5:16). However, instead of these habits helping form your relationship with God (the dos) or reflecting that relationship (the don'ts), they can inadvertently become a yardstick for how well you are pleasing God.

▶ Have you experienced this or something like it in your spiritual journey? Why does it happen?

▶ Look back at the list you made earlier. What is your gut reaction to this list? How do you measure how pleasing you are to God?

▶ What eventually happened to your list? Do you still try to live it?

▶ If you were helping a friend who had just come to Christ, how would you advise him on walking in holiness without inadvertently teaching him to evaluate how God sees him based on his ability to "keep the rules"?

▶ How does our study of Romans 6:22 from the last session inform the way we confront the frustration of trying to please God on our own?

FROM THE BIBLE

Read Romans 7.

► In what ways does Romans 7 say that the law is good (vv. 7–13)?

The law, for all of its intrinsic good, does not have the power to save us. It tells us what to do but does not empower us to do it.

► What is your first reaction to this statement? Are you surprised?

Paul says that sin actually tries to use the law against us. When the law tells us not to covet, for example, it produces in us all kinds of covetousness. Surely you have experienced wanting something the moment you are told you can't have it!

► What is the most recent example that comes to mind of this happening in your life?

► Have you seen a posted sign that made you want to do just the opposite of what the sign said? If so, please describe your experience.

Sin uses the law to deceive us by causing us either to think too highly of ourselves or to condemn ourselves based on our performance. Sin also deceives us into thinking that the law is unreasonable and God is a cosmic killjoy.

▶ How have you seen these types of deception play out in your life? Describe how sin used the law to deceive you.

Paul uses the analogy of a marriage to describe our connection with the law. We were at one time bound to the law the way a man and woman are bound together in marriage. And it wasn't a happy marriage because it involved lots of dos and don'ts. But a marriage covenant only lasts until one of the parties dies. As we already studied, when Jesus died, we died with Him because we are in Christ. He died to the law, so we died to the law. Now we are married to Christ in a love relationship, not a duty-driven relationship. Our goal is to honor and please Him.

▶ How does this analogy about marriage help you understand the difference between being under the law and being under grace in Christ? Try explaining this marriage analogy to someone right now (or write it as if you were).

► Can the law apply to a dead person? How does knowing that you are dead to the law set you free to serve Christ with a new set of motivations?

► Christians, even mature Christians, tend to default to living as if they are married to the law again. Why do you think this happens? How has this happened to you?

► How would you advise a Christian friend to live under grace instead of the law? What would you tell that person if you saw him or her bound up with rules?

► Trying to please God by our own efforts robs us of joy. What else does it steal from us?

BELIEVE FOR CHANGE

We will either go the way of the law or the way of love. Anyone who tries to follow the law to be good finds it a self-defeating experience. It just isn't enough. We become exhausted with our fruitless efforts until we give out and are unable to move forward.

Seeing elderly couples care for each other is a good example of going the way of love. One will sit at the bedside of the other for weeks or care for the other for years, not out of the strength of their wedding vows but out of love. They do it not because they made a solemn commitment decades ago but because they are motivated by love. And in acting out of love, they fulfill the law without effort.

▶ What are some rules or laws you still want to follow (dos and don'ts)? How can you now do those things in freedom, motivated by love?

The secret of the Christian life is not to master the rules but to fall more deeply in love with Jesus. In Paul's frustration at trying not to sin and failing, he finally falls only on Christ: "Thanks be to God through Jesus Christ our Lord!" (Rom. 7:25). It is all about falling in love with Christ and what He accomplished for us.

▶ What stirs your love for Christ? What moves you to worship? What provokes you to tell someone about Jesus?

Perhaps through trying to follow the law and perform for Christ, your love for Christ has been put on the back burner. Jesus Himself said that if we feel we have lost our first love, we should repent and go back and do those things we did in the beginning (Rev. 2:5).

▶ What are some things you did at the beginning of your walk with Christ that were so thrilling? Which would you like to do again this week?

▶ Write out a short letter to yourself that you can read when you feel as if you aren't doing enough to please God. What are some declarations you could daily reflect on to help you walk in freedom? Use what you studied today to help yourself remain in the way of love instead of the law.

IN MY LIFE

Take a moment to close your eyes and ask the Lord to speak to your heart as you respond to the following questions.

▶ What stands out to you from the study this week?

▶ What adjustments will you make in your life because of what you have learned?

▶ How will your relationship with God and your relationships with others change?

NO CONDEMNATION

THIS SESSION IS a companion to chapter 14 of *Soul Set Free: Why Grace Is More Liberating Than You Believe.*

FOCUS IN

▶ Have you ever worked hard to reach a really challenging goal? How did you feel when you finally arrived?

A PERSONAL WORD

Though I have climbed a few mountains before, I decided on a whim to climb Mount Rainier during a sabbatical one year. The night before my adventure Debbie, who was staying with a friend and not climbing, suggested that I do a little research about what scaling this 14,410-foot mountain might involve. When I leisurely googled it, my eyes widened and my stomach tightened. The harrowing descriptions kept me awake that night.

The next morning the outfitter told us about people who

had died on the climb and had us sign a waiver. We roped ourselves together in groups of four and practiced using our ice axe in the event of a fall. The first day we climbed to 10,500 feet, then rested for a few hours so we could get up at 1:00 a.m. and traverse the ice fields while they were still frozen. In the dark, tied to three people, I began the climb. We crossed a crevasse several hundred feet deep in the dark. As we ascended, my ice axe was in my left hand, and to my right was a several-hundred-foot drop. The path was no wider than eighteen inches in some places.

During the last hour and a half, we encountered sixty-mile-per-hour winds and blowing snow. Several times I wondered, "Why am I doing this?" I imagined at my funeral somebody saying, "Well, at least he died doing what he loved," and I thought to myself, "But I don't love this *that* much!"

As treacherous as it was, getting to the top was nothing short of euphoric. The view from the top, along with the sheer exhilaration of making it there, provided a feeling and perspective that few things in life can match.

The journey in Romans that Paul has taken us on mirrors this. We have trudged in the deep crevasses of sin, through the treacherous lows of our existence. We have climbed through the controlling power of legalism and seen how even the good law of God cannot bring the freedom our souls so desperately desire.

But then, in Romans 8:1, we reach the top of the mountain. This is where the path was always leading—the pinnacle of Paul's argument and the high peak of human existence. Enjoy this moment. Don't rush past it. Lay down your gear, breathe deeply, open your eyes, and let yourself take in the view from the top as these words wash over you: "There is therefore now no condemnation for those who are in Christ Jesus."

REFLECTION

In our last session we felt the weight of the law and our efforts to fulfill it. We acknowledged that we do what we don't want to do because sin uses the law to deceive us and rob us of joy. Now we read that there is no condemnation for us in Christ Jesus! Rightly understood, seeing the truth of this verse is like watching a million fireworks go off in front of you.

▸ What is condemnation? What do you think it meant personally to Paul when he wrote this? What does *condemnation* mean to you?

Most Christians know this verse about condemnation is powerful, but not all truly experience its power. Because it seems too good to be true, sometimes we make an amendment to this verse. Instead of reading it as "no" condemnation, we read it as "less" condemnation.

▸ If you are honest, which of the following words would you put in this blank to describe how you really feel?

"There is therefore now _____ condemnation for those who are in Christ Jesus."

- • no
- • a little
- • sometimes
- • less
- • lots of

- none or lots of, depending on how I'm doing
- (Choose your own word or phrase that best describes your experience.)

In Romans 8:1 Paul isn't describing the future in heaven after you die. He isn't saying that when you get your act together, you will have no condemnation. He is talking about the here and now—from the second you got saved until today. There is not and will never be any condemnation for those who are in Christ Jesus.

▶ When Paul says no, he means no. Have you ever given a really definite, won't-change-your-mind-no-matter-what *no*? Provide an example from your life of a no-way, never, under no circumstances, ixnay *no* answer that you have given.

You have been completely removed from the realm of condemnation, so it is impossible for you to be in a state of condemnation in your relationship with God. It just cannot happen. But since you are better acquainted with your brokenness than God's goodness, you need to be loaded for bear if you start to feel condemnation.

▶ When do you usually feel condemnation? Give some examples. What is your usual response to it?

Let this Scripture be your response to every lie and accusation of the enemy, including condemnation. "There is therefore now no condemnation for those who are in Christ Jesus." You can even read him the address: Romans 8:1. You are in Christ, and there is no condemnation for those in Christ Jesus.

FROM THE BIBLE

Read Romans 8:1–4.

Being in Christ doesn't mean you are perfect or will never sin again. It does mean that if you sin now, you don't sin against the law because He died to the law. Instead you sin against love.

▶ What do you think does it means to sin against love not the law?

Sinning after becoming a Christian is like a husband or wife who has done something to hurt his or her spouse. We don't intentionally hurt those we love, but our actions can break someone's heart. But because of the trust and love in a healthy marriage, we can ask for forgiveness and try to do it better next time. Though we may sin as Christians, we immediately seek forgiveness and ask for God's strength to avoid that sin next time.

▶ How is this like your relationship with Jesus?

Last week we talked a lot about the law of sin and death. Now Paul mentions it in Romans 8:2: "For the law of the Spirit of life has set you free in Christ Jesus from the law of sin and death."

▶ Is this scripture in the present tense or the past tense? What does that mean for you?

We know from our previous study that being set free has already occurred in our justification. God did for us what we could not do for ourselves and what the law could not do for us. But we get in trouble when we try to do analyze ourselves too much. Our eyes are then on ourselves and what we did or did not do. To live in the power of no condemnation, we must keep our eyes on Jesus and what He accomplished for us.

▶ In a moment of sin or condemnation are you focused on yourself? What would it be like to shift your focus to Jesus instead? What might be different in how you respond?

You will have good days and bad days, but the basis of your confidence will never be in yourself but always only in Christ.

▶ Romans 8:4 tells us to "walk not according to the flesh but according to the Spirit." What does *walking according to the flesh* mean to you?

▶ *Walking according to the flesh* doesn't mean gross sin. It just means trusting our own actions (following the law) to save you. Though Paul has talked about this before, he mentions it again here. Why do you think he keeps repeating this?

We weren't set free from slavery to go right back into bondage. In Galatians 3:3 Paul reminds us that we start this Christian life in the Spirit, but sometimes we go back to the flesh to live it. Later he reminds us, "It is for freedom that Christ has set us free. Stand firm, then, and do not let yourselves be burdened again by a yoke of slavery" (Gal. 5:1, NIV).

▶ Sometimes certain things draw us from freedom back into bondage. When does this happen to you? How can you sustain your life of freedom in God instead?

BELIEVE FOR CHANGE

▶ What is something that has weighed you down in the past that has come to your mind in this session? How can you leave this behind you now and turn the page on it?

▶ What is one thing you learned in this session that frees you and that you will take with you?

▶ Every chapter in Romans that we have studied builds the case for justification through grace, not by following the law. What is a concept or idea or truth that has come up several times in this study that you are finally grasping and internalizing?

▶ What difference will this truth make in your relationship with God?

▶ What difference will it make in your relationship with yourself?

IN MY LIFE

Take a moment to close your eyes and ask the Lord to speak to your heart as you respond to the following questions.

► What stands out to you from the study this week?

► What adjustments will you make in your life because of what you have learned?

► How will your relationship with God and your relationships with others change?

A NEW WAY OF LOOKING
AT THINGS

THIS SESSION IS a companion to chapters 15 and 16 of *Soul Set Free: Why Grace Is More Liberating Than You Believe.*

FOCUS IN

► Describe a time when things were so beyond your control that you had to throw yourself completely onto the power of the Holy Spirit. What happened?

A PERSONAL WORD

When I was twenty-two and married with a six-month-old, I became the pastor of a rural church. Its reputation was not promising, with the two previous pastors having short and troubled tenures. In my first few weeks there it seemed as if my story would end as theirs did. I had to step delicately through a tragic death, a charlatan guest preacher, and a large salary cut based on the fact that they were behind on mortgage payments because of a loan they took out to pay the previous pastor. Soon one board member resigned, another threatened to beat me up, and another told me he didn't vote for me and didn't want me there.

I was young, naive, inexperienced, and in over my head. But precisely because I knew I was unqualified and facing an impossible situation, I desperately leaned on the Holy Spirit. Miraculously grace took over. The Spirit began to move in unexplainable ways. Within a year we paid off all the church's debt, attendance more than doubled, and new people were coming to Christ every week!

By the time we left that church, we had become so attached to the people that it took us a year and a half to get over having to say goodbye to them. That was the supernatural work of the Holy Spirit!

REFLECTION

▶ The Holy Spirit is our Advocate, working on our behalf. Satan is the accuser, blaming and faulting us. In the previous story what are some accusations that Satan may have used against Pastor John? What are some ways the Holy Spirit advocated for him?

In this study we have laid the foundation of salvation, including forgiveness, grace, justification, and faith. It is important that you understand and grasp each of these because the foundation is what everything else is built on.

▶ In a nutshell, explain what you have grasped so far about each of these foundation stones.

- forgiveness

- grace

- justification

- faith

In Romans 8 we see God the Father, Jesus the Son, and the Holy Spirit working together for your salvation. Paul begins to talk about the role of the Holy Spirit. God's plan is not for you to work out your salvation by your own effort or resolve or work. He has planned for the Holy Spirit to do the heavy lifting.

▶ What does that mean to you? How is that a relief to you?

Life with God is about cooperating with the Spirit, yielding to the Spirit, and allowing the same power that raised Jesus from the dead to work in you, through you, and for you. You become a dwelling place for the Holy Spirit the moment you are saved. The Spirit is at work in you all the time—when you are praying, sleeping, working, and doing everything else.

▶ The Holy Spirit works in you and with you in many ways. Describe how you have experienced the Holy Spirit in these ways:

- strengthened you

- changed you so you are like Christ

- empowered you

- revealed the heart of God to you

- led and directed you

FROM THE BIBLE

Read Romans 8:5–17.

► Based on this passage, how would you describe the flesh? Do you remember our definition from the last session?

► Here are some other ways "the flesh" is translated or paraphrased in Romans 8:5. Which seems the best to you? Which one speaks to you the most?

- selfishness (CEB)

- old nature (CJB)

- desires (CEV)

- sinful selves (ERV)

- corrupt nature (GW)

- lower natures (TLB)

- sinful nature (NLT)

While we look at what *the flesh* means, it is also important to exclude what it doesn't mean. It does not imply that our bodies are somehow bad. Nothing could be further from what Paul had in mind. God Himself came to earth in the man Jesus Christ, which we call the incarnation. He chose a body on purpose. Plus He interacted with bodies in all states: touching lepers, applying mud and spittle to a blind man's eyes, and healing a woman with an issue of blood. Then the body of Jesus was torn and mangled on the cross, and that same body was physically resurrected.

▶ In what ways have you felt that the body was inherently bad? How has that negatively affected you?

For Paul, flesh is shorthand for a life that is disconnected from the source. Living according to the flesh is living by desires that have not yet been altered by grace. It is following your most primal instincts and seeking what you want at the expense of others. The flesh's priorities are pleasure and feeling good rather than God, the things of God, and the people of God.

Though we live in these fearfully and wonderfully made bodies, we do not have to obey their every whim or desire. In fact, after becoming a Christian, many of the desires we had before fade away and are replaced with new redeemed desires.

▶ What are some examples of this from your life or the life of someone you know? What have you noticed that you no longer desire, and what has that been replaced with?

Being a Christian is like having your default settings changed so you have a new normal. If there is a tie in your life, God wins it. When we prioritize the things of God, sometimes we have to say no to sports, recreational activities, and social functions that interfere with important gatherings of God's people.

▶ What are some areas in your life in which there are ties? What change can you make in your life so that God wins the tie in these cases—so that choice comes from your heart rather than from a set of rules?

▶ Paul said that life in the flesh is hostile to life in the Spirit. What does that flesh-versus-Spirit reality look like in your everyday life?

We do not have to live according to the flesh because, as Paul said, "All who are led by the Spirit of God are sons of God" (Rom. 8:14). Of course that means both sons and daughters of God. We don't have to fall back into fearful slavery because we are now children of God through adoption.

Think of it: God adopted you. Adoption is a legal action by which a child is taken into a family and given all its privileges. During Paul's time an adopted child actually had more privileges than a biological child.

It was common in the Roman Empire for a man to adopt a son, perhaps because his own children weren't worthy or up to the task of managing his estate. Several of the Roman emperors were adopted sons: Augustus Caesar, Tiberius, Trajan, Hadrian, and Marcus Aurelius. An adopted child was chosen with intention.

► How was adoption in Paul's day different from today? Why might being adopted as a son mean more to Paul's original readers than to us today?

Several things happened with adoption in the Roman Empire. First, the adopted person lost all rights to the old family and gained all rights in his new family. Second, the adopted person became the full heir to his new father's estate, even if there were other sons. Third, his old life, including debts he owed or crimes he committed, was completely wiped out.

► What are the implications of the results of the Roman adoption in thinking about how God has adopted us into His family?

Even today when a child is adopted, a new birth certificate is issued with the adoptive parents' names. When God adopts us, we are accepted as His children in every way.

► Jesus stated in John 17 that the Father actually loved Jesus' followers even as He loved Jesus (v. 23). How does this truth have deeper meaning to you now?

The Spirit of God bears witness in us that we are God's children. The spirit of slavery has been done away with. Our old anxieties have been replaced with a childlike intimacy with God whereby we call Him "Abba! Father!" This is a term of endearment similar to "Daddy!"

Since we have been adopted into God's family, we can walk by the leading of the Spirit instead of the impulses of our flesh. We have God's Spirit living in us to empower us to do this.

BELIEVE FOR CHANGE

▶ What is your greatest personal battle between the flesh and the Spirit?

▶ If you had to teach someone what it means to walk in the Spirit, how would you describe it? Give a few everyday examples.

▶ Not all of us had fathers who make God the Father look attractive or trustworthy to us. You may have suffered neglect or abuse, or you may have had an absent or a withdrawn father. Even the best fathers can leave us with a deficit because no one is perfect. Which of these do you feel you need most in your relationship with your heavenly Father?

- comfort

- protection

- acceptance
- provision
- safety
- quality time
- affirmation
- encouragement
- tenderness
- attention
- strength
- honesty
- dependability
- other: _____

▶ Write out an honest prayer to God, asking Him to begin healing your image of Him. Ask Him to show you how He is already doing those things you chose from the list.

IN MY LIFE

Take a moment to close your eyes and ask the Lord to speak to your heart as you respond to the following questions.

▶ What stands out to you from the study this week?

► What adjustments will you make in your life because of what you have learned?

► How will your relationship with God and your relationships with others change?

GOD IS WORKING
IN ALL THINGS

THIS SESSION IS a companion to chapter 17 of *Soul Set Free: Why Grace Is More Liberating Than You Believe.*

FOCUS IN

► Can you describe a situation in your life in which you had to wait patiently, and maybe even painfully, for the beautiful outcome to happen?

A PERSONAL WORD

I'll never forget the first time I ever preached on a Sunday morning. It was September 30, 1984, and the reason I remember is that Debbie was pregnant with our first child and started having contractions the day before. Once we got to the hospital, they decided she wasn't ready to give birth. Only after our pleading did they reluctantly give her a room. Debbie's contractions had almost completely stopped.

Right there and then Debbie and I knelt down and prayed for the baby to come before noon. In less than an hour the contractions came with intensity.

Though we had gone through birthing classes and I knew my role, nothing really prepares you for the experience of a woman giving birth. My job was to help Debbie control her breathing, so I hovered over her face, telling her in a smooth voice, "Debbie, you have to breathe. This will help you!"

Instantly she looked back up at me and said, "Would you please be quiet!" There was only so much comfort I could provide Debbie at that moment in the midst of volatile, intense, painful labor. Thankfully our son was born healthy on September 29!

God is in the process of completing the work of making us new. This is at times painful for us and can involve suffering. But like the pain of childbirth it is temporary. This pain is minuscule compared to the beauty that awaits us.

REFLECTION

We learned in the last session that we have been adopted as sons and daughters of God. And the time will come when we gain our full inheritance. But meanwhile life is messy and suffering is real. We are in the in-between time. We are not promised an easy, carefree road. Suffering, as well as glory, is part of the Christian life.

► What are some ways that life gets messy and full of suffering? In our families? With our faith? In our bodies?

▶ Jesus promised us that "in this world you will have tribulation" (John 16:33). That's not a promise we usually claim. Paul called the suffering he went through to take the gospel to people who had never heard it "light momentary affliction" (2 Cor. 4:17). List some of his light momentary afflictions from 2 Corinthians 11:24–33.

Paul added that these sufferings were "momentary" and not to be compared to the "eternal weight of glory" that was coming (2 Cor. 4:17).

▶ How does this inspire you to press on through suffering and the difficulties of life?

Some kinds of suffering we experience don't seem to have a sense of meaning or purpose unless they are understood in the context of the long game—what God is doing in eternity. If this life was all we had, many of our troubles would have no meaning. But as Christians our trials are placed against the larger backdrop of where God is taking us. Suffering takes on a sense of purpose it could not have had before.

▶ Difficulties in life are inevitable, but why does it help to know that they won't be wasted or meaningless?

Creation groans and we groan in this broken world. We can't outsmart the pain or outrun it. But we can look forward to the redemption to come. As our groaning increases, so does our hope. This life has its limitations, but there is the promise of another, eternal life. God is birthing in us the desire for heaven, the desire for home.

▶ How can you comfort yourself knowing that the best is yet to come?

FROM THE BIBLE

Read Romans 8:18–30.

One of the most treasured verses in all Scripture is in this section: Romans 8:28. The promise that "all things work together for good" is a promise for believers, a hope reserved for those who are in Christ.

▶ What does "all things" mean?

God can take even your sin, temptation, disease, abuse, mistakes, and tragedies and leverage them for your good and for His purposes.

▶ Which of the items in this list surprises you? Did you know that God can even use that?

Nothing is too dark or difficult for God to harness, leverage, and repurpose for good. He can take the dissonant notes and use them in writing His beautiful symphony. He brings beauty out of brokenness. Henri Nouwen taught that God actually heals through our wounds, just as God brought us healing through the wounds of Jesus on the cross.[1]

► What is your gut reaction to that statement? How have you experienced that kind of healing?

God can take ugly things, which will never happen in heaven where His will reigns, and transform and transfigure them so they bring healing and wholeness to those who are facing them now. Paul went through hardships in Asia that led him to even despair of life (2 Cor. 1:8). But God comforted him in his afflictions so he could comfort others with the comfort he received in his time of need (v. 6).

► Have you noticed that God often uses what people learn through their most painful experiences to help others through those same difficulties? Give some examples.

► What are some tough experiences that you have gone through that God might use to help others?

► Sometimes when we think of things working together for good, we think of perfect Hollywood endings. Add to this list some non-Hollywood ways that God can work things together for good in your life.

  • Make you more dependent on Him.

  • Bring healing to your soul.

Paul says that God foreknew you and predestined you to be conformed to the image of Christ, "and those whom he predestined he also called, and those whom he called he also justified, and those whom he justified he also glorified" (Rom. 8:29–30).

It all begins and ends with God. He loved you beforehand, He chose you, and He called you. You heard Him whisper your name, and you answered. He justified you and clothed you in a robe of righteousness, covering all your shame. You were forgiven and given a new identity with a new nature and a clean slate. And finally you will be glorified.

► How does it feel to you to know that God chose you, called you, and has a future for you?

BELIEVE FOR CHANGE

▶ What is something that you once believed that God could never use for good? Why did you believe that? How has that changed after this session?

▶ What are you suffering right now? Which of these truths helps you the most as you walk through this with God?

- This will work together for good.

- This is a momentary affliction compared to eternity.

- Joy is coming and it will last forever.

- This is helping me depend on God.

- This experience will make me able to help others.

- God will use this to finish His work in me.

- Other: _____

▶ How can you remember these things as you go through the messiness of life?

▶ What is the most freeing truth you have grasped during this session?

IN MY LIFE

Take a moment to close your eyes and ask the Lord to speak to your heart as you respond to the following questions.

▶ What stands out to you from the study this week?

▶ What adjustments will you make in your life because of what you have learned?

▶ How will your relationship with God and your relationships with others change?

MORE THAN CONQUERORS

THIS SESSION IS a companion to chapter 18 of *Soul Set Free: Why Grace Is More Liberating Than You Believe.*

FOCUS IN

► When was the last time someone accused you of something? Whether the person was wrong or right, how did being accused make you feel?

A PERSONAL WORD

I hope you have enjoyed this journey through Romans 1–8. Though Romans is a brilliant book, it would be tragic to see it as "heady" when it is foremost heart. Through Paul's words we see the heart of God, a God who knows everything about you—the good, the bad, and the ugly—but loves you anyway. For all the insight you may have gained about justification, sanctification, and glorification, I hope that most of all you walk away with a profound sense of the soul-freeing power of God's grace.

God is for you. He chose you and loved you before you took your first breath. God went to the length of sending His Son to take your place on the cross, becoming sin for you, so He could bring you home to be with Him.

It is grace that made you aware of God's love and drew you to receive God's gift of salvation. It is a grace greater than all your sin. You are not condemned and will not be condemned because you are in Christ Jesus. The Spirit lives in you, is at work in you, and is changing you.

Celebrate that grace, grow in that grace, and rest in that grace. It is not only greater than your sin, but it is grace that will lead you home.

REFLECTION

► When you look back at who you were when you started this study, what changes do you see in how you view grace?

► What benefits have you seen in your life and relationships from those changes?

► Think of a recent situation in which you applied a truth you learned from this study. What happened?

► How would you describe this study to your best friend? Why should your friend begin this study on Romans?

► How has your relationship with God changed?

FROM THE BIBLE

Read Romans 8:31–39.

Paul began Romans 8 with the declaration that there is no condemnation for those of us who are in Christ Jesus (v. 1). As we come to the conclusion of this chapter, Paul, like a brilliant attorney, makes his closing argument for grace.

Paul had experienced accusation, mocking, torture, opposition, and persecution. Yet he begins this closing with saying, "If God is for us, who can be against us?" (v. 31). No matter who else is against us, God is permanently, completely, and irrevocably for us. He has already decided to be on our side forever.

► In which area of your soul do you need to breathe in this truth? Why?

As proof, Paul reminds us that God didn't even spare His own Son in order to rescue us. If that's the case, how would He not give us everything else we need (v. 32)? There isn't anything He wouldn't do for us when He has already done the ultimate. There is nothing He would withhold from us when He has already given His best and His all.

▶ How can you internalize this truth so that you never doubt God's love for you again?

Though we receive this as truth, we know our own hearts. We know what it is to feel accused, blamed, and ashamed. Though we may face accusation from others, our greatest accusation comes from ourselves. Plus we have another accuser—Satan. Accusation is who he is and what he is. And he has good ammunition to use against us—our mistakes.

Just when we start to listen to Satan's accusations or our consciences accusing us, Paul shoots back, "Who shall bring any charge against God's elect? It is God who justifies" (v. 33). The heavenly court is open to hear charges against us, but none will stick. God is our judge, and He has already justified us. The punishment for all our sin was placed on Jesus. Our debt has been paid.

▶ From this we understand that it is impossible for the God who justified us to bring charges against us. How can you convince yourself of this truth?

The more we remind ourselves of who God says we are, the fainter the voice of the accuser becomes. The day will come when "the accuser of our brothers and sisters, who accuses them before our God day and night, [is] hurled down" (Rev. 12:10, NIV). Then his voice will be silenced completely.

▶ Did you breathe a sigh of relief when you read that? How can you remind yourself that you actually live in that freedom now?

God is fully acquainted with your failures and mistakes. He sees your every mangled motive and all your self-deception. Yet he knows the sacrifice His Son made for you was enough, and He loves you completely.

While God is justifying us, Jesus is interceding for us (Rom. 8:34). Because Jesus was tempted as a man, He is sympathetic to our weaknesses. Jesus is your Advocate, your Defender, the One who pleads your case. Just as He did not condemn the woman caught in adultery (John 8:1–11), He will not condemn you. Jesus is willing to stand between you and your accuser. He always has your back.

▶ Have you ever felt that Jesus was accusing you? What do you believe now?

The evidence of God's love for you is overwhelming. Paul concludes his argument by proclaiming that nothing can separate you from God's love in Christ:

Not trouble, not hard times, not hatred, not hunger, not homelessness, not bullying threats, not backstabbing, not even the worst sins listed in Scripture: They kill us in cold blood because they hate you. We're sitting ducks; they pick us off one by one. None of this fazes us because Jesus loves us. I'm absolutely convinced that nothing—nothing living or dead, angelic or demonic, today or tomorrow, high or low, thinkable or unthinkable—absolutely nothing can get between us and God's love because of the way that Jesus our Master has embraced us.

—ROMANS 8:35–39, MSG

▶ Put your heart of praise into written words!

BELIEVE FOR CHANGE

You are permanently, desperately, and entirely loved.

▶ Are you convinced that God can overcome any scheme and attack that comes against you?

▶ Are you persuaded that God is for you, that He is on your side?

▶ Do have the assurance that He is not accusing you or condemning you?

▶ Are you sure that nothing and no one can ever separate you from God's love?

► Are you confident that God will complete the work He started in you?

► Are you finally persuaded of God's love for you through His grace?

If there are any obstacles still in your way, deal with them now by answering these questions:

► Have you repented of your sins and fully received His forgiveness?

► Are you living in the assurance that you have right standing with God because of what Jesus did for you on the cross?

► Are you trusting only in God's grace and not in anything that comes from yourself?

► Have you accepted all these truths in faith?

Finish with a prayer of thankfulness to God.

► Who will you tell about this new freedom you have in God?

IN MY LIFE

Take a moment to close your eyes and ask the Lord to speak to your heart as you respond to the following questions.

▸ What stands out to you from the study this week?

▸ What adjustments will you make in your life because of what you have learned?

▸ How will your relationship with God and your relationships with others change?

NOTES

SESSION 2: THE BEST NEWS YOU'VE NEVER HEARD

1.   Johnny Cash with Patrick Carr, *Cash: The Autobiography* (New York: HarperCollins, 1997), 169–71, https://www.amazon.com/Cash-Autobiography-Johnny/dp/0060727535.

SESSION 3: THE BAD NEWS

1.   C. S. Lewis, *The Great Divorce* (New York: HarperOne, 2001), 75, https://www.amazon.com/Great-Divorce-C-S-Lewis/dp/0060652950.

SESSION 6: DEAD TO SIN

1.   "Frances Havergal Wrote 'Take My Life and Let It Be,'" Christianity.com, updated June 2007, https://www.christianity.com/church/church-history/timeline/1801-1900/frances-havergal-wrote-take-my-life-and-let-it-be-11630571.html.

SESSION 11: GOD IS WORKING IN ALL THINGS

1.   Henri J. M. Nouwen, *The Wounded Healer: Ministry in Contemporary Society* (London: Darton, Longman & Todd, 1994), 88.